Thinking About You

Thinking About You

A New Interpretation Of Our Bible

PAUL THOMAS WENZLER

Copyright © 2020 by Paul Thomas Wenzler.

ISBN: Hardcover   978-1-6641-3402-7
               Softcover   978-1-6641-3357-0
               eBook   978-1-6641-3356-3

All rights reserved. No part of this book may be reproduced or transmitted in any form or by any means, electronic or mechanical, including photocopying, recording, or by any information storage and retrieval system, without permission in writing from the copyright owner.

Any people depicted in stock imagery provided by Getty Images are models, and such images are being used for illustrative purposes only.
Certain stock imagery © Getty Images.

Print information available on the last page.

Rev. date: 10/02/2020

To order additional copies of this book, contact:
Xlibris
844-714-8691
www.Xlibris.com
Orders@Xlibris.com
818914

CONTENTS

INTRODUCTION

Have you ever considered why the Messiah was so put out with the religious leaders of his day? He called them hypocrites, at his mildest. It wasn't just that, all men are hypocrites! He was frustrated because they not only wouldn't enter into the healing processes he was prescribing, but that they also purposely were keeping out even those who desired to be saved. In the religious efforts at preaching life after death, that very idea was the impediment that kept everyone from exploring what salvation might mean and how it applies right now to everybody. When he was told by a man who complained that he didn't have time because he had to attend a funeral, the Messiah responded, "Let the dead bury the dead." His message wasn't about what the preachers preached.

The problem with religious leaders is twofold: One, they are paid to find salvation and are given all the free time in the world to do so, but they don't! And two, most people don't have the time or the resources to spend their days in prayer and exercises and so are dependent on how best to proceed getting on with their lives, even though they suffer tremendously just to keep body and soul together. If religious leaders could find their own way, then maybe they really could become teachers and guides at helping their followers find their own peace and salvation. You know, at the end of Revelation, after peace is restored and salvation has returned to the earth, the necessity of a church or a religion is over. When salvation comes, we're all "human beings" once more, connected to our living bodies. That's a promise our God will keep.

How do I know all this? I learned from practice and having a good teacher. You might tell me that Christ is my only teacher, and I couldn't agree more. But first, you have to get in touch with that teacher inside of each body, and that is how I began practicing, practicing what my mentor Thomas Merton called silent prayer and my instructor called meditation. You can learn all this yourself. And the best place to learn is from Jon Kabat-Zinn's book *Full Catastrophe Living*. Where I began was with the Veteran's Administration hospital program, and it totally changed my life. What was missing was my poor connection with my living body, and over time, that was healed. What I will argue in this piece of writing is that is exactly what our Bible is testifying has happened within our "being" nature, and the solution is a return to our bodies. I wish everyone God speed on their return to this new adventure of coming to life again, renewed, so to speak.

One more thing I forgot: In the text, when the man of Eden was told that he couldn't care for and nurture his garden responsibility solely by himself, I wrote that he couldn't do that alone. That's true, but I should have put that in plain words. He couldn't do that without a *body*, and that's true! You see, *That was the problem!*

IN THE BEGINNING

A lot of people are anxious and worried right now for their health; for the economy; for basic services like housing, food, and income; and for their future on the planet with so much trash constantly being dumped in bigger and bigger spaces everywhere and over the unending destruction of environments across the whole planet! All this is on account of us, people, everywhere! We're all in and on this together, you know? But here's the problem: Our species is divided among ourselves and inside ourselves. This has been the case forever! Don't kid yourself. We, all of us, need to wake up to some facts about our nature. This pandemic has everyone's attention, and it's highly recognized how important working together is right now. But we're not! Why is this? It's the divide in our "being" nature! (Genesis 10:25)

So here's where I introduce to you Sergeant Pepper's Lonely Hearts Club band. You wish. It's *the Bible*. It's our wake-up call. And how is that so? It not only tells us of "the divide" but also how to become undivided, i.e., whole again. Wholeness is peace; division is suffering. Also, the good news is this: everybody is well prepared right now to wake up in their body.

MY IDEAS ON THE BIBLE

Our Bible needs one more interpretation. You see, the Bible's meaning remains a mystery to most believers. They don't get it, not that they might agree with me about "not getting" it, but because religious people's lives are predicated on ignoring the feelings of their very bodies. And it's not just them by any means. We're all guilty of this. And without understanding the glitches in our behaviors, there's no way to regain our lost nature, which is the Bible's sole objective. So it might be more enlightening if I present a simple overview of our Bible from the beginning to the coming of Abraham. Human beings aren't stupid unless you're referring to the traumatized people with PTSD symptoms. "Stupid" comes from the Latin *stupidus*, meaning *to be stunned*, to live in passivity and fear. There's a lot of that in the population, unfortunately.

I believe just explaining those opening chapters can open the eyes of anybody who might want to hear the Bible's message. Also, religious leaders of the three Western religions need to wake up to the Bible's message and turn the course of religion away from waiting until we've died to healing the bodies we have now. The truth will do that. And right now, I think we could really use something as good as a spiritual awakening in all peoples on the planet to restore hope and begin watering the seeds of love. I mean, our human being nature is good. God made it! And by retelling the Bible's opening passages, I'm going to give our Bible a much needed final interpretation. Put the message in everybody!

My source for all quotes and the stories themselves is the Jerusalem Bible Reader's Edition. This translation has been touted the best since the King James Bible. And I believe its English is more than proficient to explain itself. Is it true to the original texts? All the experts say it is.

First, I want to begin by generalizing from the big picture and then breaking that into smaller and smaller pictures, showing more detail, and only so far as to make the picture clear. Let's be clear: The Bible isn't the solution nor is the picture it presents; both are depictions of the present condition of our being nature. The solution is a shift in perspective and the awakening of an inner awareness that every living body possesses and the acknowledgment, as is said at the beginning of mindfulness classes, that there is more right with you than what's wrong and we're going to address what's right with you. This allows for a return to biology or, in the Bible's terminology, the rising from the dead. In the beginning, our nature, human being nature, had become corrupted and then lost from personal awareness, and everyone had to flee from her or his body. Bodies had become unsafe. That holds true to far too many places on the planet right now.

Our Bible begins with mankind, which was the third generation[1] in our being nature, but "in the beginning," that nature had already died in the prehistoric great flood. This is presented in the second line of the book of Genesis: "Now the earth was a formless void, and There was darkness over the deep, and God's spirit hovered over the waters."[2] I'm just going to look at the first twelve chapters in the book of Genesis, from the beginning up to the coming of Abram or Abraham. I'm looking for what happened to have caused so much suffering?

[It might be helpful to have an actual text in front of you as I proceed so you can see for yourself. Or maybe not! Just gallop through

---

[1] Just as bodies change from childhood to boyhood to adolescence to adulthood, so too change our minds. Being is a state of mind. These unique mindsets were termed generations in the Bible, with their own lifetimes, and yet these lifetimes were continuous with older generations. The third generation was the adolescent mind.

[2] This is creation having to start over *again*. Creation, in our being nature, is going on all the time!

and see what you feel. Personally, I prefer the latter plan. Myths are tedious.]

The Big Picture or How Our Bible Begins

1. First is the seven days of creation. God makes our human being nature. Earth and heaven are part of that nature. Man is part of that nature, made in the image and likeness of God and his spirit. The seven days ends with Sunday, when God rested. God rested because his creation was good. In the beginning, which begins in the aftermath of the flood, God remade our indoor nature and saw that it was good.

2. The second creation, man is made from the soil of the earth.[3] Also, the garden is made, woman is "enclosed in flesh," and the man loves up to his partner in a little poem about how wonderful she is. This all culminates in two scenarios answering some "this is why" head-scratcher.

3. Then the troubles: a serpent, the tree of knowledge, the temptation. You won't die? Then her eating the apple and giving it to the man to eat, and both overwhelmed by shame and the fear, a new emotion that knowledge had aroused.

4. The blame and the curses put on the serpent, the woman, and the man. How the man will now suffer horribly and never be satisfied until he returns to the dust from which he was made, i.e., until he redoes his own creation. That's what Abel means.

5. The naming of the woman, Eve, followed by the man being expelled from his paradise with his wife and a fence of living fire in the hands of baby angels is set around the garden, protecting it from the man returning. The Gods note how divided the man has become.

---

[3] I could say the soil is the environment, but it's more than that. Man is made out of his own creation. This is personal, which means deniable. Always blaming others is an easy way of avoiding one's own nature.

The word "human" being comes from the word *humus*. Earth is the source and home of this nature.

6. Now outside the garden, Eve births Cain, with the help of Yahweh. Cain is the new man. Then the child Abel is born. Because Yahweh hurts Cain's feelings, he kills Abel.

7. Cain's driven from the land and has to wander the earth, homeless and fearful of being recognized and killed for being a brother killer. He's marked by Yahweh, the spirit, so he can be recognized, and is, thus, protected by Yahweh. Cain's mark stands for seven times[4] vengeance on anyone who kills Cain! Yahweh's seen as a vengeful spirit, just like mankind.

8. Then we have Noah's dad, Lamech, killing a boy and a man. (Three "deaths" have now entered our "being" landscape.) Lamech curses anyone who wishes to harm him, like Yahweh protected Cain, to a multiple of ten times the curses put on anyone who thinks of taking revenge on him—seventy-seven[5] times! His marks were low and ineffectual because mankind won't rest until justice is replete with satisfaction.

9. The man from the garden gets the name Adam just prior to chapter 5. His name means Red Land, from the blood that cries out to heaven. This new Man, Adam, has a talk with his

---

[4] A generational lifetime is seven years. This comes from Pharaoh's nightmares. It's also generally recognized today as boundaries in both childhood, boyhood, and adolescence, ending with twenty-one when individuals are assumed responsible. Until then, they're really not responsible. What the spirit instituted, in seven times vengeance, is an eye-for-an-eye justice system. This retribution or "justice" is in our indoor nature. It's a law of that nature, like karma in Eastern wisdom. Whenever you or anybody does violence to another living organism, their living organism is damaged on the inside immediately. Where do people think "nightmares" come from, outer space? I don't think so. They come from our bodies, the one right now breathing. There's a lot we might ought to be thinking a bit more about if we truly wish to live a vital, healthy life.

[5] Now we have 777 = 21. Translated, our human being nature is either whole or completely lost. In John's Revelation, the mark of the beast, 666, translates as "incomplete" in the first three generations. Nothing of our being nature has come to fruition. And as we know from the seven days of creation, God has not rested. There's huge implications of guilt put on the Gods on account of all the violence in our world. In their own stories, "they" are the cause, meaning, the problem is in and part of our being nature. That is the way it is!

wife—Eve[6] is at this point gone—and "the wife" gives Adam a son, and this son has a son, Seth, who is the first "Man" to call Yahweh by the name Yahweh. Spirit is now in the big picture. Alone; and disconnected from his partner God, representative of the divide between body and mind. This is the divide in our being nature.

10. Enter the new genealogy, beginning with Adam, who is just like God, and now spelled "Man" with a big M, like God with a big G. And everybody to come will be like the "Man." The Man is created. The other guy in the garden, he was made from the soil of the earth. This new Man is like God, also alone. (How many men experience being "like God"? You know, in their personal heads, alone.) There's interesting stuff in the genealogy but not now. The apostle Paul, he had a big disdain for genealogies.[7]

11. The tenth guy in Adam's genealogy is Noah, the good man who "will give us, in the midst of our toil and the laboring of our hands, a consolation derived from the ground that Yahweh cursed" (5:29). Noah was the first water bearer. Noah's hope was to quell the fire resulting from the expulsion from the garden of mankind's delight. Like in the seven days of creation, night came, and so too came Noah.

12. Now there's this thing about the increased population of mankind on the earth, and they started taking, like Noah's dad did, more than one woman and Yahweh grew unhappy. He said, "My spirit (that's woman) must not forever be disgraced in man, for he is but flesh; his life shall last no more than a hundred and twenty years." These men kind were special because they were the sons of God. And they were the heroes and had the biggest

---

[6] Eve, from the text, means "mother of all those who live." When Abel was killed, Eve died.

[7] The New Testament was the Bible's first interpretation, but for the people, it was still a mystery. Our being nature, this ability of creating our own environments and the beings who populate them, remains as shady as art itself, and though the myths themselves are exactly the manifestation of this creative nature, this has not been recognized. It's in the genealogies where this generative nature is first laid out.

families on the block. They didn't care about the children; they were the celebrities. Yahweh, in the *mean*time, was "on fire"!

13. Now Yahweh says men are wicked, greatly wicked. All they think about is wickedness all the time. Yahweh was grieved. His own creation – He is THE spirit (was he also the cause? He was the cause of Cain, Eve said so) – and all the animals, even that nasty serpent. All this his own creation. Remember the Seven Days of Creation, when God said he wanted this or that? He was the motivator. He feels responsible. Then he thought of Noah and smiled.

14. Now we get Noah's story. You know, the good guy, man of honesty, like the apostle Paul, bursting with integrity, that's Noah! Noah has three sons. Abruptly, God enters the picture. In God's sight, the problem was the earth; it had become corrupted. The earth was filled with violence—men against men, against women, against everything! God thought about this. It was corrupt, for corrupt were the ways of all flesh on the earth. If we got rid of the earth? No, it's the flesh and the earth together that corrupts, God thought. Maybe we need a new earth? Was he right in his thinking? Who was there to question God's judgment?

15. God comes down and teaches Noah all about boating, you know. Three levels, three generations. He tells Noah he's going to drown the planet. He was going to turn the fire to mud. And what he instructed Noah to do with the transmigration of souls and animals in his boat you can read from the story. Of big interest, though, are all the dates, the months and days and years, 'cause in the end, we'll see that the story puts all the events in Noah's mind; and this was important because when Abram arrives, by then, we know that the real problem the Bible is addressing is the one inside skin, that no eyeball can see. But the home owner sees it, oh yeah. Don't kid yourself.

16. Yahweh returns to repeat what God says, they go back and forth, both involved, both at fault, both completely invested. The head and heart of human nature, that's our Bible Gods,

being and spirit. You gotta believe them! Or you don't. Free will, you know?

17. Then we get the flood. This is chapter 8. It's just like the second line of Genesis; now the earth was a formless void, there was darkest over the deep, and God's spirit hovered over the waters. That would be the black raven Noah released. Look it up. That's what dried up the waters. It could also be his wife (women, at that point, had a dark side), who, after the flood, is no longer present. (I mean Noah started drinking for his inspiration 'cause his wife was not happy living in a boat of animals, i.e., pent-up feelings that got no release.)

18. Noah finally lands and seems like terrified to get out and live. God had to intervene to get him out. And he empties out all his emotions to roam the earth once more. A pair of every kind that was after the first flood but "before" the one in Noah's mind! But they're all good, the first creation. What about the nasty snake?

19. Then Noah builds an altar and immediately burns up some kids, lambs, to appease Yahweh's hunger for roast lamb. Yahweh smells and promises no more flooding. I mean, how sincere is that? He's the fire spirit, like Paul promised. But now here's the latest promise. Opposites are to be forever. Good and evil are like a part of something whole, and you can't kill the part without the whole thing going belly up. Like the Christ said in his stories, be careful what you pull up, something like that. The big speech is God's.

20. God tells Noah to be a terror across the land toward all the wild beasts; don't let them bully you. Stand up, be strong against all those animals. But don't eat meat. Was God for real? Why, yeah. It's meat that has the life blood in it. Life is over when the meat is cooked. The life that's over was "being," the past tense. See, Noah didn't know about life, he was flesh himself, and flesh is the first thing to be abandoned when body pleasure is gone. "In the beginning," the flesh turned out to be evil. All the beings were leery of the flesh. We don't know "what" we are, but

we ain't *that*! The flood makes a living body forget it's a living body. Anyway, God promised never to flood the earth again, you know, the rainbow in the sky. The real problem ahead: how to get the water *off*, i.e., gone, so the circuitry works. It's not universally accepted; but we are electric beings!

21. Now we get the true consequences of the flood: Ham discovers his dad dead drunk in his tent and naked. He tells his brothers. What happened to the wife? Is she gone? His brothers don't want to know. Noah is obviously not connected. The brothers, Shem and Japheth, hide their dad under a covering. But when Noah wakes up and finds out that Ham saw him exposed, all Noah can do is curse Cain's descendants, i.e., Canaan.

22. Noah blames Canaan for all the sufferings that he's gone through. He blames Cain for the flood and the loss of everything he had. To understand, I will return to this word—understand—when we look for a second time at the seven days of creation, but for now, we must accept that our nature is divided between feeling and thought, the first-born and the second-born. Canaan is the fourth generation in our being nature, the time of thought[8] and reason. Noah curses that fourth generation of our being nature with slavery to Shem (the desires of the physical body—eat, drink, and be merry) and slavery to Japheth (the adolescent male mindset of control and power). As the text reads, "Canaan shall be his brothers' meanest slave."[9] On the other hand, Canaan becomes the object and goal of all God's promises, of restoration and wholeness. (Talk about internal tension!) The problem from the beginning was mankind's addiction to slavery and, thus, the promise to free men from their own addictions. Turns out, shame is an implacable obstacle to healing. It hides admitting the condition of my condition, which is the prerequisite.

---

[8] Two attributes of our Bible's God is all knowing and omnipresent. Both are faculties of our being nature. We all are like God, in our knowing and in our presence; but the 4th generation, in the beginning, was deeply enslaved.

[9] Basically saying the present 4th generation of males will just "hate" everybody.

23. Now comes the "peopling of the earth," the descendants of Noah's sons. It is here, under Ham's sons, that the four generations are first set down in persona or representatives: Cush, Misraim, Put, Canaan. Noah's genealogy begins with Japheth, then Ham comes second and fills up the most space, and finally, Shem's sons, who are not called sons but children. Shem is the firstborn, the Men-kind, like Adam, like God, and his firstborn will go toward the introduction of Abram after the generations go through ten new types.[10]

24. But just before that, the Babel story is injected between Noah's sons and the new genealogy. It explains "the how and why" of what prompted Yahweh to go down to the plains of Shinar and confuse mankind's language so that they could not work with one another solving problems. This is a blanket statement about the universal corruption in language across the whole species before historical times and also a warning that from a biblical perspective, language cannot solve the disease in our being nature. In fact, to enter and pass through those processes of rebirth, our thinking body has to be put aside and ignored while we learn to refocus on what our senses and the immediate environment are saying in the present moment. And in this sense, our Bible is no more than an affirmation of success if, and only if, a disciple or believer returns to her or his senses and takes up living once more in the body. In returning to my body, the totality of creation becomes present, and that includes all the personal history that is pertinent to my own unique life. Life becomes mine! Freedom now becomes possible.

I'm arguing that the first twelve chapters of Genesis lays out the problem that God of the Old Testament couldn't solve nor could his son

---

[10] This is how Judaism got stuck as a universal Western religion by proposing how and where from the twelve types of mankind originated. It wasn't from the alignment of the stars but out of the behavior and wishes of their mothers and who the mothers were in the pecking order of how things operated on the female side of life. See the sons of Jacob. 29:31 – 30:24.

in the New Testament because it all remained a mystery to the human beings of those times! What were they talking about? What is clear, though, is the continual dissemination of suffering. The divide is the cause of all suffering, but that can end. You know?

This quest on my part to find a solution to the biblical quandary began in 1990, while reading RG Collingwood's *An Autobiography*. I had no idea at the time what I was actually doing. I had just gone through a divorce and was looking for some way to quell the hurt. What was wrong with me? I had turned to Collingwood, looking for answers. What I got was the question "If the Gospels are given as the solution, then what's the problem?" Even at that time in my beginning, awakening life, I just assumed it had to be at the very beginning of our Bible. Like every good story, the problem has first to be made plain, to be laid out before our eyes. Our being nature is awesome at problem solving, once it's turned on.

In the opening myths of Genesis, the word *created* is hugely important. I can't know the minds of those early translators of the Hebrew Bible into Greek[11], but *created* in Greek has its root in their word "flesh." Flesh and death has long been recognized as the problem in our Bible, although our Bible's death isn't synonymous with flesh. (That's the quandary in religion.) Our minds can run away from the flesh easily. It's called transcendence! But here's the dilemma: According to the book of Genesis, God put our being nature and all its universes in the flesh. Like it says, "In the beginning, God *created* the heavens and the earth." Just to be sure, they could have ended their opening line with "in the flesh." Yeah, right. Who would believe that? But back then! I mean, we don't know how our ancestors understood those stories. We're guessing all the time. But modern neuroscience would agree: Mind and body are one "in the flesh." A mind and a body can't be divided out of each other; that's science. It's also research and proven to be the case by experiment.[12] This mind/body image is the same man/woman image

---

[11] The Septuagint Bible.
[12] See Jon Kabat-Zinn's *Full Catastrophe Living*.

in the Genesis story of the Garden of Eden, and the impetus of that story is that "being" is our own creation. As spectators, people who live outside of life, usually in their own ideas and aspirations, these Bible stories are what life is like in our being nature or was at one time in everybody's life. Our Bible says that what once was is also right now. Right now is everything!

No matter how weird or scary the idea of living in my own flesh body is, there will be no peace in the whirlwind of my mind until the marriage of man and woman is once more pieced together in my awareness. And the one big promise of both testaments is peace!

A LITTLE BIT CLOSER

Some interesting things about the seven days of creation begins with the initial statement: Let there be light, and there was light. From the creation of day one, it is easy to assume that the light comes from our sun because also on day one comes the night; both words in everyday usage. But the sun is actually implied when God made the two lights set in the sky, but those lights have another meaning that I will mention when we come to day four. The light on day one is "understanding," like seeing what you're standing on, what's under foot. This could also be named "knowing." In any case, neither word is used. Light *is* the word. Light makes us happy; arrests our anxiety. The light was said to be "good." And it stood apart from the darkness. Christ, in the NT, was said to be the light. Light, for the cornerstone of well-being, is *everything.*

On day two, God wanted a vault to separate the waters, to be a safe place that water couldn't get to. This vault was called "heaven." If you had a place in heaven, a flood was never a threat. Someone could've told the guys at Babel that they didn't need a tower to get above the waters; they needed a vault. Also, we could tell everybody you don't need to die to go to heaven, just go to your nature because heaven is already made and there. And it holds all your loved ones. That's day two.

On day three, God wanted some dry land under heaven for his own creation to feel safe and have a place to call home. And there it was. God called the dry land "earth" and the surrounding waters "seas." God saw that dry land was "good." God wanted things to grow and food to eat on the earth and fruits to tell the truths of what the trees were all about. We get our word "true" from our word "tree." By eating the fruits of a tree, we know the truth about our nature. These plants were seed-bearing, carrying the ideas of truth into the next generation. And so it was. That's day three.

Now we come to day four and the two lights in the vault of heaven that shine on the earth. (Note that the lights are in heaven already.) These lights are to govern the day and the night and to divide light from the darkness. These lights, according to our Bible, are your mom and dad. They're the ones who set our habits and ideas in orbit that govern my ways and our activities. We honor our father and our mother because they're the cause! To understand this, we turn to the Joseph story and his dreams. I'm going to just mention the subtle issues, but you can read the entirety in Genesis 37:2-11.

"He (Joseph) had another dream which he told to his brothers. 'Look, I have had another dream,' he said. 'I thought I saw the sun, the moon, and eleven stars, bowing to me.' He told his father and brothers, and his father scolded him, 'A fine dream to have!' he said to him. 'Are all of us then, myself, your mother, and your brothers, to come and bow to the ground before you?'" Jacob clearly understood the imagery.

Our being nature is reflective; it makes images from the body's sensations and then charges them with emotion, bringing them to life inside that nature. When we're tired, when we're angry, when we want this or that, an image pops up, and we "know" what to do, what we want, without even raising a question. Our being nature maps the whole world without us rising a hand. Know thyself, and this is what you discover. This is the power of imagination dressed in language, the image made into the word, like pizza! You cannot only see it and taste it, but you can also smell it and feel how heavy it is! Everybody is a sense animal endowed with "being." Charles Darwin understood this!

On day five, God wanted the seas to come alive, and so he "created" the great sea serpents and every kind of living creature that teem in the waters. They come with the flood and then live inside our seas for us to know! This is how Jonah got eaten by the leviathan and spent three nights in total darkness until he was vomited up on the shores of

Nineveh and saved those people on the verge of losing their town. You know what it's like to have a whole *town* of your being landscape just blown to smithereens? Think about that. And in heaven, he created the birds, translated: *and in the vault he released some ideas.* These birds could also turn fierce, like what they did to Pharaoh's baker and how they were about to pick the flesh off Abram's heifer, goat, and ram that he'd cut in half and hung up in making a deal with Yahweh to ensure his success upon entering the Promised Land until he chased those black birds off. Bible birds can be some "bad" ideas that it doesn't pay to keep in anyone's heaven. Just remember who put them there and figure out a way to let them out of your vault. And that ended day five.

Day six was "the" big day. God made all the animals and breathed into them, and they became living beings also. The animals are beings that roam across my lands and the emotions of being alive that I feel whenever certain images appear on my landscape. These are the drivers of the sense world. And God saw this was good. Then he got down to business and said to his spirit, "Let us make man in our own image, in the likeness of ourselves, and let them (males and females) be masters of the fish of the sea, the birds of heaven, the cattle, all the wild beasts, and all the reptiles that crawl upon the earth." *Let them be masters!* Masters are kings and queens. And God promised Abram that Sarah's offspring would be kings, and in the NT, over the crucified Christ, the placard "King of the Jews" was hung. The King is with us in our shared being nature. You don't have to worry!

We run again into the word *created* here three times. "God created man in the image of himself, in the image of God he created him, male and female he created them." Not to be overly picky, but my "being" man by the text is both male and female. Our being nature is replete with opposites; just like in the real world, there are two sexes. In me, two sexes too. This is where "God-given" beings come from. You know?

It's out of this inner duality that came the "person" I identify with, the actor who I am. A God-given offspring, the second-born!

The sixth day ends with God blessing man, saying to them, "Be fruitful, multiply, fill the earth and conquer it. Be masters of the fish of the sea, the birds of heaven and all living animals on the earth." God continued, "See, I give you all the seed-bearing fruit; this shall be your food. To all wild beasts, all birds of heaven and all living reptiles on the earth I give all the foliage of plants for food." Sounds to me like God is saying, "Don't eat one another!" On the other hand, for mankind, their food is truth. Without truth, how does a body know? And so it was. God saw all he had made, and indeed, it was very good, thus ended the sixth day.

Chapter 2 opens with a summary. Heaven and earth were completed with all their array. And God rested. He blessed the seventh day and made it holy because on that day, he rested after all his work of creating. Such were the origins of heavens and earth when they were created. Again, the word "created" is twice used.

Remember, keep holy the seventh day! This was one of the Ten Commandments. Why? So that we don't forget, one, that God's creation (our "being" nature) is good and, two, that when it was completed, God rested. So what went wrong and what are we to know or to take away from knowing what went wrong? By seeing, inhabiting our body, the light of understanding will come on, and a "fix" will appear. Creation once more will work, and we can return to delight. And foremost, our Bible God can rest.

Yahweh blamed himself for making mankind, and then he set about destroying his own creation. From the Bible's perspective, Yahweh is the source of all our suffering. If it is fixed, then Yahweh might just stop destroying it (which translates to "so might I stop destroying my own life!"). That's the Bible's message for Jews and Christians and the hope in our faith, a faith based on the cessation of suffering.

In Genesis 2:5, the second creation myth begins. Two things are notably different: One, the creator God is named Yahweh God. This is the first instance of the name "Yahweh." Let's quote, "At the time when Yahweh God made earth and heaven there was as yet no wild bush on the earth nor had any wild plant yet sprung up, for Yahweh God had not sent rain on the earth, nor was there any man to till the soil." God, in this instance, is the father of our being nature, in our image.[13] Yahweh is his partner and spirit, the spokesperson for the wife, who is about to enter the picture.

And two, in the beginning, God created the *heavens* and the earth. In the beginning, the heavens are plural, more than one, or one for every mankind. When setting out to make a man, the myth opens with one earth and one heaven for one man. The story is now personal, about one actor[14] they call man with a little "m." The next line begins: "However, a flood was rising." This flood is hormonal. Remember, this man is the protagonist in the third generation of our being nature, and this myth is about the "making" of him. He's not "created." He's made. His body has always enclosed him, although he seems not aware. How could he be? He's in the middle of creation and has been for the past two generations, childhood and boyhood. This is a whole new experience because of hormones, which translate into passions, the deepest of emotions, which live in the sea of his being nature. In the waters, implying the elements of our spirit's life sustaining resources, live our passions!

So it begins; Yahweh God fashions man out of the dust from the soil and then "breathes" into his nostrils a breath of life, and thus, the man becomes a living being. Breathe is what beings do. Breath is our connection to body. The teenager is *now* a living being. Then he's forgotten for a while, kind of left standing there breathing and, like many teenage boys, in awe, if not in outright terror. "What is this place? How'd I get here?" to quote David Byrne of the *Talking Heads*.

From these opening creation myths, we know that our being nature is about making everything we "sense" into words and then language, thought! Experience defined. And it's all made out of imagination, the faculty that translates sensation and charges it with emotion. That's the power of being, the nature of mind and spirit, in the image and likeness, most notably, of our parents; but that's just the personal, immediate experience. Our being nature is as old as mammalian life and, totally

---

[13] Image, or the picture of being, is whatever mind state that individual occupies in the present. God is however your mind imagines. There's no permanency.

[14] We get our word "person" from the Latin *persona*, which means actor. Acting is always temporary and impermanent, that's the good news.

wise, connected back to life's beginning. The Eastern religions all say the same thing: Become aware, and you will understand. Wake this nature up. It's alive and always present. It's our heritage. Over here in the Occidental, we've been a bit slower waking up! Always doing, that's us; and right now, overdoing is the real death threat. We can't stop!

Right now, in the story, the man's asleep. So they, God and his spirit, or Yahweh God, go about building the whole thing over again. They plant a garden they call Eden. Eden means "delight." Whether from the light or for the pleasure of making, delight encompasses both. And into delight they put the man. Now, with the flood rising, all the living trees that are truths spring up for the man to eat and to look at because truth also is delight. In the garden's middle are two trees of the utmost importance, the tree of life and the tree of the knowledge of good and evil.

A river flowed from Eden, my delight, to water the garden, and from there, it divided into four streams. Some proper names now enter the story. The first stream is named Pishon, and it encircles the whole land of Havilah, where there is gold. The gold of this land is pure; bdellium and onyx stone are also found there. Havilah shows up as the second-born of the sons of Cush in Ham's genealogy. This is the first generation. In the gospels, when Jesus is born and the magi bring gifts, gold, frankincense, and myrrh mimic the wealth in the first land of Eden. And in Pharaoh's dreams about the plight of the land in Egypt, the first generation is rich and abundant. Childhood is the first generation, the mother/child generation.

[In Ham's genealogy, this mother/child image is gone. Cush, who we're about to come to, is all male, ruled by Yahweh. This is because by Noah's time, the mother image, Eve, will be gone, along with Abel, the child god. I'll come to this shortly.]

The second river is named Gihon, and this encircles the whole land of Cush. Cush is Ham's firstborn in that genealogy. The second generation of our being nature is iffy, exemplified again in Pharaoh's dreams. Famine, in the story of Joseph and Pharaoh, is the subject matter of Pharaoh's two dreams. In his dreams, everything living withers and dies across the lands. That's Pharaoh's nightmare; the second generation wasn't flourishing! Egypt represents the second generation under Ham's genealogy, under the name Misraim.

The third and fourth rivers are the Tigress and the Euphrates; no lands are mentioned. These would be the third and fourth generations. Creation now isn't about fundamentals, thus no lands, but worlds made for living. Life is established in the first two generations; now it's up to beings to sort and direct. Like the question "What do you want?" this seems to be the implication of the text. Although this directing and nourishing isn't done alone, the dominant factor becomes inspiration or spirit. So we study the names of the rivers of these two generations. Tigress is a female cat of great ferocity, especially around the protection of her young. This is the spirit source for the third generation. Would that be Yahweh?[15] And the fourth, Euphrates, means "the good waters," the nomenclature for the generation to come.[16] See, mankind was an intermediate generation and due to pass with the arrival of the last generation, fatherhood. But first, the man had to die again.[17]

"Yahweh God took the man and settled him in the garden of Eden to cultivate and take care of it. Then he told the man: 'You may eat indeed of all the trees in the garden. Nevertheless of the tree of the knowledge of good and evil you are not to eat, for on the day you eat of it you shall most surely die.'"

That is the death the Bible is hoping to put an end to forever, the one that came with the knowledge of good and evil, the knowledge that we are broken. That is not true, but our being nature dies if separated from its partner, by losing its connection to the living body. The three

---

[15] When Israel blesses Jacob's sons at the end of Genesis, he says, "Judah is a lion cub . . . like a lion he crouches and lies down, or a lioness . . ." 49:9.

[16] "The Spirit and the Bride say, 'Come.' Let everyone who listens answer, 'Come.' *Then let all who are thirsty come:* all who want it may *have the water of life, and have it free.*" Revelation 22:17.

[17] "In the beginning," he was dead. Under Ham's genealogy, his third son was named Put. Put meant nothing. That was the plight of the third generation at our Bible's start. To return the man to life wasn't recognized until the New Testament. The Christ came to show his disciples the "way" back to life, which was named the way of the cross. That's scary! How enticing is that? Here's the good news: The cross is your own "living" body! How wild is that?

major Western religions[18] are the consequence of this knowledge, really, of death. But they've blinded themselves about this death and what that means.

Then Yahweh God said, "It is not good that the man should be alone. I will make him a helpmate." Our species seems plagued with loneliness and depression, and it's why we seek companions and soul mates. The above line isn't about finding another body. It's about finding a mate for our being nature. And that mate, it turns out, is the flesh[19] body, mother nature. Why are we so indifferent to the environment? It's pretty obvious, isn't it? We aren't connected to our own bodies. We don't know them!

The story tells of Yahweh God making all the animals and bringing them before him to see what he might call them, giving every being a name. This is hugely important if we are to be "masters" of our being nature because it implies "knowing" everything in that nature intimately. But no beings were found to be a suitable mate for the man. So he put the man to sleep, took a rib from his breath, and enclosed it with flesh. He brought this to the man, and he exclaimed, "This at last is bone of my bones, and flesh from my flesh! This is to be called woman, for this was taken from the man." Loneliness problem solved! Now our garden man has a body, which isn't only emotional. It's a sensation. Who'd have thought? Still, Mr. Kabat-Zinn likes to explain it's not what you think!

It's noted in my text the play on the words "man" and "woman," making a joke out of taking woman from the word man. The reverse is possible, but the man had become overly excited just imagining woman coming out of *him*, so crazily happy was he. Well, look. "You can't get no woman out of man." What is possible, not just in language but also in physics, is that man (this being nature) came out of the flesh body.[20]

---

[18] Religion comes from the Latin *religio* and means to bind back. The implication is the man and woman reunited.

[19] The word is a pejorative, indicating self-loathing, but in actuality, our life source is the miracle of the natural world.

[20] The immaculate conception and incarnation, it started with the man's little poem to his body, their body!

This is supposed to be self-evident. Obviously, nobody got it, especially men-kind, which includes priests. They're men too, aren't they? We're all in this together.

Now we get two very important statements: "This is why a man leaves his father and mother and joins himself to his wife, and they become one body." And "Now both of them were naked, the man and his wife, but they felt no shame in front of each other."

I go now to the prophet Malachi (2:10-16): "Have we not all one Father? Did not one God create us? Why, then, do we break faith with one another . . . ? It is because Yahweh stands as witness between you and the wife of your youth, the wife with whom you have broken faith, even though she was your partner and your wife by covenant. Did he not *create* a single being that has flesh and the breath of life? And what is this single being destined for? God-given offspring. Be careful for your own life, therefore, and do not break faith with the wife of your youth. For I hate divorce, says Yahweh the God of Israel, and I hate people to parade their sins on their cloaks, says Yahweh Sabaoth. Respect your own life, therefore, and do not break faith like this."

I mean, what do you say to that?

Now we arrive at the most controversial piece in the whole Bible: the fall of mankind! I'm not about to try and explain what the serpent stands for or exactly what is going on. You know, and you don't know! The picture is just too huge. But some things are without a doubt, like where this fall and expulsion story is heading. It's heading toward death, suffering, and slavery, ending this intro piece of our Bible with Noah cursing our being nature and hating mankind and leaving all bodies in despair. That's where this is going. The events detailed are all part of our being nature body and a most recent part too. And they are repeated over and over in every new participant that falls out on the planet through the love and labor of each new mother who gives birth, with one exception: the Bible's story is about the second-born, the cause of our suffering.

In our story, the bad guy is the serpent. He is a liar, for one thing.[21] He's also a misogynist. He's a part of the male being nature that blames all our suffering on the flesh body, and when that body's dead, good riddance— He's angry for reasons that only a snake might know. Snakes have never been well thought of by human beings. They're underfoot, and they bite!

Another factor, looking at a snake flat across the ground, he's powerless to rise up, unless someone like Moses does it for him. So what's he good for? The Garden problem seems to reside around the question of where's the offspring? Is the man a failure? Are the snake and the man one? Barrenness plaguing the wives of Abram and Isaac was the *big* issue in the re-beginning. How are beings actually made?

Whatever the explanations about who the actors are, the consequences of being tricked by the serpent are spelled out. Separation, expulsion, and suffering are the consequences of eating of the knowledge of good and evil. The fall, like the flood, is before historical times and so is buried in our being nature, in our living bodies. A body doesn't have to fully know why it feels a certain way, but acceptance begins the healing processes and opens the door to changing those feelings. So what happened? What are we asked to accept? For one, nobody's life is easy.

The fall story opens with this line: "The serpent was the most subtle of all the wild beasts that Yahweh God had made." Now a dialogue begins. Not much different from any moral debate that goes on in our heads when we want something that we ought not have.

The serpent asks the woman, "Did God really say you were not to eat from any of the trees in the garden?"

The woman responded, "We may eat the fruit of the trees in the garden. But of the fruit of the tree in the middle of the garden God said, 'You must not eat of it, nor touch it, under the pain of death.'"

---

[21] In the New Testament, everyone knows who the devil is. He's an incorrigible liar! He's the opposite of "I am the way, the truth, and the life." Devils cause people to burn, like the experiences of Cain. Molech of the Old Testament is another example. He abused children.

The pain of death is exactly what would worry a flesh body, like my body. But worry is a mind disease, isn't it? Knowledge is what a mind wants; fruit is what a body wants. Are the two different sides of the same want? And by the way, God didn't say any of the above things exactly.

Then the serpent said to the woman, "No! You will not die! God knows in fact that on the day you eat it your eyes will be opened and you will be like gods, knowing good and evil."

What does the serpent want? And why is he angry? Why does he yell at the woman? Those exclamation points mean he's threatening her. This serpent's a bully! What's his problem? His problem is that he's a serpent and has a split tongue. Serpents talk out of both sides of their mouth. And the reason he's that way is he too was made by our being nature, to talk on whatever side of an issue was most attractive to him. God made him just like that, and he doesn't like it. He must believe, like our minds say they believe when facing frustration and failure, that if we knew the truth, we could become something else by our own smarts. He's hungry for *knowledge* so he can *rule*! Life rules, not the actors on the field.

Now the woman is tempted because it has been suggested that eating what is forbidden will exempt her from the pain of death and she will be like God. She's already like God, but at this point in the beginning, she doesn't know that. What does that mean, to be like God? Is it to be a creator? For sure! But "knowing good and evil"?

So she ate. Then he ate. Then their eyes opened, and they both saw the other, in each other's unclothed body. Like Noah, drunk on the floor of his tent, the man's manhood was flat on the ground, like a serpent. The man no longer felt any attraction for his flesh body because he realized it was "evil." But they hid their understanding behind the leaves of the fig tree, a sweet smile. This is the shame that's so impossible to bring into the light. And there was one more awesome reaction: fear!

A new dialogue begins with Yahweh God calling to the man: "Where are you?" he asked.

"I heard the sound of you in the garden," he replied. "I was afraid because I was naked, so I hid."

"Who told you that you were naked?" he asked. "Have you been eating of the tree I forbade you to eat?"

The man replied, "It was the woman you put with me. She gave me the fruit, and I ate it."

Then Yahweh God asked the woman, "What is this you have done?"

The woman replied, "The serpent tempted me, and I ate."

Being is a state of mind in the present moment, filled with the feelings that brought this state into existence. So is our serpent. But there are feelings in our being nature which are *not* to be acted out because they *will* cause long-term suffering and alienate us from life itself. That is why this creator God curses the serpent's mindset: "Because you have done this (distorted the truth), be accursed beyond all cattle, all wild beasts. You shall crawl on your belly and eat dust every day of your life. I will make you enemies of each other: you and the woman, your offspring and her offspring. It will crush your head and you will strike its heel."[22]

Then the woman is told of the consequences of introducing the divide between our two natures into life. "I will multiply your pains in childbearing, you shall give birth to your children in pain. Your yearning shall be for your husband, yet he will lord it over you." It seems to me our minds are uncomfortable with their own bodies and often are loathed to pay attention to what's bothering them; nor do they care to listen to those consequential rumblings coming out of bad decision makings. This kind of mindset, "lording it over the body," doesn't bode well for an individual's future. In truth, the mind/body relationship isn't divisible. This internal tweaking is more illusion than truth. If you pay attention, you know.

____

[22] I remember as a kid one of the statues in our church was of the Virgin Mary standing on the head of a serpent. The above line was its inspiration. The statue stood for something else, something more immediate, more real. Make the human physical body strong, and it will crush all its enemies. You can depend on the foot of Mary, everyone's living body. Mary means young woman, the name the man gave his partner in the garden.

And then the man is chastised for listening to his body when he already knew that that knowledge was not for his well-being or health. (What about young men in seminary learning about good and evil, which the church does teach, right?) "Because you listened to the voice of your wife and ate from the tree of which I had forbidden you to eat[23]: Accursed be the soil because of you. With suffering shall you get your food from it, every day of your life. It shall yield you brambles and thistles, and you shall eat wild plants. With sweat on your brow shall you eat your bread, until you return to the soil, as you were taken from it. For dust you are and to dust you shall return."

It's for this reason alone that religious traditions bury their dead in the earth, but the whole import of these curses bear testimony to the corruption in our language and our being nature, the nature of knowing, cognition. This isn't about aging bodies but the diseases in thoughts and feelings, and these the consequence of separation. This is why we suffer and can't get our lives in order.

The garden story ends with a summation. "The man named his wife 'Eve' because she was the mother of all those who live." It's past tense. And her name will only be used for Cain and Abel, then it will disappear at the same time the man will get his name. What does Eve mean in the story? It's not hard; our being nature comes from our physical body. The physical body is our mother or the mother of our being nature. When Abel is killed, what then? What does a death mean to a mother? Does it matter? The story is quiet on that because the mother is gone.

But ask any woman today. Does it matter? I think the future of our species depends on it because it means that the love and care between

---

[23] You see, with the liars' help, the man tricked the woman into helping him do what he had already been wanting, to become like a god and live forever. In fact, he was never in any way connected to his woman, so this whole scenario was inserted after the fact in hopes of showing men kind that it wasn't their fault exactly, *but* it needs to be fixed! The men these stories were addressing, unfortunately, were long lost and didn't have a clue how creative their indoor nature really was. No different with the men of today. That's why these myths are so in-your-face blatant and a lot of good that's done, right?

our living bodies and our minds, that faculty that *rules* our behaviors, is now nonexistent. That's what Eve means!

Yahweh God made skins for the man and his wife, and they put them on. Now they are two, disconnected, no longer with "one body." Each has her and his own. Duality, in the real world, is everywhere you look, competing for survival, and guess who loses out? The easy answer is every "body." Historically, women and children have been the big losers. But in the coming new time, in the book of Revelation, John sees an age with females restored to their partnership with males. This is presented by the number of elders singing about the child's holiness. (4:4) There are twenty-four elders: the twelve kinds of males with their partners, the twelve kinds of females; now twenty-four beings!

Yahweh God speaks: "See, the man has become like one of us, with his knowledge of good and evil. He must not be allowed to stretch out his hand next and pick from the tree of life also, and eat some and live forever." So the story says Yahweh God expelled the man from the Garden of Eden to till the soil from which he had been taken. "He banished the man, and in front of the garden of Eden he posted the cherubs, and the flame of a flashing sword, to guard the way to the tree of life."

The man's alone again. The woman remains in the garden. The woman is his body. He's got his wife, she comes along with him, and he talks with her, and that is how he figures out what has happened. (All this is a live picture of the processes of our creative being nature actually at work, or storytelling at its best!) Cain is what has happened. Eve conceives, after having intercourse with "the man," and she tells him the conception wasn't *his* fault. Yahweh helped her. The man out of the garden had nothing to do with conceiving Cain. Cain means "forged in fire." That flaming sword on the garden's perimeter burned somebody, and Eve said it was Cain.

Another fact—Yahweh now is by himself. So too is God. They've come apart, like the man without "his" woman. Next, Eve gives birth to Abel, the child. Nobody helps Eve with Abel. Cain is the new man. As Eve explained in her own words, "I have acquired a man." Cain and Abel are disparate generations in our being nature, and their stories are highlighted so we see the different generations. Being is knowing, and what mankind is now knowing is death. That's what the knowledge of good and evil is about. Its true knowledge is not good to be dead. It's a feeling experience. What enters with this knowledge is fear, and fear is what shuts down living, which is how the religious got accused of being dead and why the coming of Christ became essential for resurrecting dead beings back into living bodies.

The Cain and Abel story is well-known, but it's not really. Myths are packed with information that supersedes the simple sentences. First, the proper name Abel means *father* (Ab) *of God* (El). El was the God Christ calls out to on his cross. El is short for Elohim and is used to distinguish God from Yahweh. I've read it means God is gracious. This is the highest state of being: fatherhood—representative of a concerned and loving care giver, totally involved. A fatherhood in partnership with motherhood and a communal connection to both the environment and all the stages of generational development in our being nature. Abel to be a god any child would love. How could such a deity come from a child's conception? Imagination! Imagination is the child's mind. This all-loving image of God is the child's making, and it's not hard to imagine. Superstition is also the product of imagination, often the consequence of fright or abuse. In the child's mind, sensations can be huge and powerful events from which children need affirmations and the securities of mature caretakers, something that was completely and totally missing "in the beginning." This needs to be spoken loud and clear everywhere the Bible is cherished. In the beginning, there were no fathers to love and care for their children! Remember Christ saying "Only the Father is good."

Back to the account.

Abel is a shepherd, while Cain was a farmer. So there's a party, and the two bring their produce as offerings to Yahweh, the Lord of creation. Abel offers the fat and the healthy, the firstborn of his flock. This pleases Yahweh. He likes Abel's offering but not Cain's. Yahweh didn't like Cain's offering of brambles and thistles, which is all a farmer could grow in the soil, since it was cursed. So Cain kills Abel. Whose fault is this? Obviously, it is the fault of whoever cursed the man, which would be Yahweh God. That's why Yahweh felt bad and tried to protect Cain, although now Cain was completely banished from the land, another immigrant. That's today's Cain, but the one in the story eventually settled in Nod, east of Eden. The ancients equated sleep and death in our being nature as synonymous, characterized by invisibility or non-presence. Who me? Cain wasn't stupid though. What follows his banishment is the Bible's first genealogy, a genealogy of beings.

The storytelling is brilliant, the opening line: "Cain had intercourse with his wife, and she conceived and gave birth to Enoch. He (Cain) became a builder of a town, and he gave the town the name of his son, Enoch." So first off, Cain talked with his wife. That's how beings communicate. They need words since "reading" another body has become like impossible. Body language died when we abandoned our bodies so that we might participate in the rapture with *God*! So Cain's wife asks, "What's going on?"

"Well, the whole world hates me and are out to kill me, and I don't know where to live, and farming's out, and I'm really scared for my life . . ."

So this is what Cain did: He built himself a town, called the town just like he called his son and took up living there in his son's generation. I mean, the man degenerated back into the boy and chose to stay there. So did everybody who followed, all ten of them. And their names, from the research I did on proper names and their meaning, many carried warrior connotations, like javelin thrower and good with sword, etc. After the flood, war was the new normal. (Look at any world mythology, it's always war or war-related.) And then the genealogy comes to Noah's dad, Lamech. Lamech took for himself two women, and like Cain, he too lives in the second generation. These two genealogies are about the son's time. On one side are the sons of man (beings), and on the other, the "sons of God," who are Adam's descendants.[24] Anyway, Lamech takes two women, and they have two lineages of beings going down different roads. One lineage are artists, and the other are metalworkers

---

[24] Scholars tell me the two genealogies are of the same guys. Like I need a scholar to see the story.

and iron guys, with sisters who could make even ole man Noah rise from his stupor. But then Lamech did a nasty! He kills a boy and a man and curses everybody who might want *revenge* to the tune of seventy-seven times worse punishment on anyone who thinks of harming Lamech. Noah's not even mentioned until the next genealogy. But before I leave, one thing is noteworthy: This genealogy on "beings" isn't about dying; nobody mentions that. I mean, these guys were without bodies, so why die? They come from nothing (a little dirt), are nothing (Put), and then go right back to being nothing, like the breath leaving a body; not so with Adam.

Being isn't a physical state, though it absolutely is embodied. And in that body, excess water (hormones in the bloodstream) can be a real problem. The problem is like shorts in an electrical system, more like disconnects, across the living body; not dissimilar to losing your Internet connection—your world goes dark, like Ham. The transmigration of the soul across the divide between generations never arrives and is presumed to be lost at sea! That can happen.

A little pause here. Our being nature is creative. This should be self-evident since creating is exactly everything our Bible Gods are constantly doing, and we're just like them.[25] And that is what the story of Lamech with his two wives do—make beings with "talents." That's the two lineages, one musicians and the other craftspeople, with talented females to boot. Everything we have today is because of the creativity in our being nature. This makes full circle back to mankind's *delight*; creating is the light of our nature.

Right after Lamech has sworn seventy-seven variations of vengeance on the whole world, the first word in the upcoming sentence is Adam. Adam means red land. The land now has the blood of three generations on it. So everybody coming after Adam, made in his likeness, has blood on their lands. Our being nature is passed down through each

---

[25] The corruption caused by the knowledge of good and evil is that the dead see everything as "sexual" and sex as the great quandary in the world, which is just another way of saying woman. The knowledgeable believe sexuality is totally God's domain when it's not a biblical issue at all. The problem is upstairs, with our heads. Christ died at Golgotha, which means "skull."

generation, and this nature is "long-lasting," close to forever. And its reach is across the whole universe but only in the present. Being is always here and now. So people don't know unless they enter now. Adam didn't know because Adam was like God in being without a partner, i.e., woman, in the first language. Everybody who came after Adam, they didn't know either. And that's why, collectively, we suffer.

You see, Adam drown in the flood, not Noah's flood but the one at the beginning, when the earth was a formless void and there was water over the deep. His genealogy says Adam lived for some hundreds of years, having sons and daughters just like him, who didn't know too, and then he died and was put in the dirt and decomposed and then later put into some other body and breathed into, and there he was again, just recycling dirt, and he didn't know it. He thought, "What's the purpose? Kids? What?" Viktor Frankl hadn't yet written his book, having survived yet another genocide. Men can't get enough hating, can they?

I'm making light. What's interesting in these two genealogies is that the generational maturity is stopping pre-puberty, in the second generation. That's exactly what the story, the one following Adam's genealogy, is about to tell us. "When men had begun to be plentiful on the earth, and daughters had been born to them, the *sons of God*, looking at the daughters of men, saw they were pleasing, so they married as many as they chose." I think I've been over that, and I need to turn to something which is of more importance and can easily be overlooked: the time line in Noah's life and events. The story says that when Noah was five hundred years old (it started taking longer and longer for mankind to make sons and daughters in their spitting image), he became the father of three. This was heralded a miracle! That's a joke. Before Noah, it was one son; Noah made three. He broke the mold.

Three was as far as the generations had gone. The fourth generation was unknown. There were no fathers, just boys and teenagers. In the New Testament, the third generation was called perverse.

I'm going to do some jumping around now to highlight the place Noah's flood fits into our being nature. We know the causes that roused the gods to destroy their own creation, the degradation of women and forcing them into roles of subservience or worse. Can you see how that would cause wars from the incensed sons of these mothers? Think of Ishmael. Then there's the violence men used to ensure control. Violence is the most destructive of intrusions into our being nature since it obliterates the connections we need in making meaningful choices and keeping free from self-doubt and incrimination. The end of all violence is the best hope for universally regaining our being nature.

And isn't violence against all moral law? What is wrong with our "godly" people is that they don't demand justice against all who harm living bodies. Don't they feel it?

So Noah's time line. As was already said, when Noah was five hundred years old, he became the father of Shem, Ham, and Japheth. "Noah was six hundred years old when the flood waters appeared on the earth" (7:7). "It was in the sixth hundred and first year of Noah's life . . . when the water dried up from the earth" (8:13). Now we go to the patriarchs after the flood and read in the account of Shem, who leads the new genealogy. "When Shem was a hundred years old he became the father of Arpachshad, *two years after the flood*" (11:10). When Noah was six hundred years old and the flood began, Shem was one hundred. After the flood, with the starting of the genealogy that will introduce Terah and his three sons Abram, Nahor, and Haran, two years have gone missing. Those two years are in the firstborn's history. That would be the body's history, what it experienced on the inside. The flood was always in the being landscape, not the body's sense-scape.

Something else turns up missing from Shem's descendants under the big picture of Noah's genealogy.

"Shem also was the father of children, the ancestor of all the sons of Eber and the elder brother of Japheth." (Shem is the firstborn and, therefore, the conduit through which our being nature is transmitted.)

"Shem's sons: Elam, Asshur, Arpachshad, etc." (10:21, 22).

The flood breaks the "life connection" to older generations. The individual becomes divided. Shem is the example. Arpachshad is Shem's third generation. Again, let's follow the text. "Arpachshad became the father of Shelah, and Shelah became the father of Eber. (He was just mentioned in 10:21.) To Eber were born two sons: the first was called Peleg, because it was in his time that the earth was divided . . ." (10:24, 25). The earth is the ground of our being nature. The divide has gone into our heads, cutting off experiences from older lifetimes that might be pertinent for exercising wisdom in present situations, i.e., for "knowing" how to be. In Shem's account, that knowing are his children.

What was the life connection that Shem lost and, thus, lost to all future generations? They lost the nurturing and care of the first two generations.[26] In Shem's genealogy, Elam and Asshur are those generations. Elam means the land of El or God. That would be the Garden of Eden. And Asshur, he would be the builder of the great cities as told above under Cush's descendants (10:11, 12).

This is the Bible's account of how our "being nature" got lost from our memories and why we continue to suffer in our lifetime. Everything in the Bible from this point on makes no sense in language since man and woman are no longer defined the way they were at the beginning since the language is about our indoor nature and because all the big and important words most often used are taken to be historical events of another time and having nothing to do with my indoor nature right now, which remains mostly dark. So talking to you about the rest of the Bible is, at best, going to be middlingly dissatisfying because we can't agree on the meaning of the words since God confused their meaning.

I've no idea where this should end. There are a zillion things that could be said, like the promises of a new heaven and earth found in Isaiah (at the end of chapter 65) and at the end of John's Revelation. But in my mind, the most pressing transformation needed within our species is a universal conscious return to our living bodies because it is there we will once more rediscover what it means "to be." And peace is the reward for coming home to our body. Isn't this what religious people the world over seek in their quest for salvation? I believe it is!

Is there a plan? There is!

---

[26] The first effort to address this issue is in the story of Joseph and Pharaoh, following Joseph telling the pharaoh about his dreams' meaning. And then came the Joseph law meant to address the famine or how to help the kids stay whole.

RIGHT NOW!

You know something's going on here, but you really don't know what it is. Do you? Mr. Jones.

                           —B. Dylan

"You know!" Usually, this is uttered by a speaker trying to quell an anxiety attack and a little flummoxed over where or how to begin. But in my case, it's a statement that everybody does know and the nervousness that comes with walking on shaky ground. How'd I get here?

Unfortunately, knowing also comes with a lot of ambivalence because of the divide between sense and feeling and the subtle differences surrounding the two. Nor does it help when a lot of people are hell bent on ignoring everything around them, including what's happening inside their lives. But I can hear what you're thinking and you're gonna say I'm dreaming.

I can easily predict that the second coming of Christ will happen quite quickly once it's gotten into the public mind what our Bible is about. But not right yet because our Bible remains a mystery, and this condition of ignorance is confounding. To be confounded is to live inside a state of confusion and suffering.

But I think most bodies know things are not right everywhere. And this is nothing new. This blind groping about in search of peace and a life worth living has been ongoing throughout history. Nothing is ever "right," right? There's always that little bit that's askance, if not a whole lot wrong. These hard times had their beginnings with the advent of knowledge, which we remember began with language. "In the beginning was the word and the word was God." Language and God, in the Western spiritual mind, are closely intertwined. Then something happened that caused a great flood, and according to the book of Genesis, *God* came down and confused mankind's language. What happened, according to the book of Genesis, is mankind had refused to "partner-up" with life, and this was why God did what he did. That's what the Bible says. Knowledge then became the words that appeared in ideas, and some of those ideas could really make you sick. Sick is the most basic symptom of suffering. Language did that!

Our Bible, in the beginning, warns mankind, "Don't eat from the tree of knowledge of good and evil 'cause if you do, *surely you will die.*" Knowledge became the cause of death, not the death that renders the body cold and lifeless but the kind of death that allows passion and ignorance to kill the soul. That is the death the Bible promises to end. Anytime we're ready, it's a promise that's for real; no more souls need ever die again.

"Soul" is an interesting word. It's of English origin (which means it's a new concept or idea) and is said by my dictionary[27] *to be* "the animating and vital principle in man credited with the faculties of thought, action, and emotion and conceived as forming an immaterial entity distinguished from but temporarily coexistent with his body." In the Genesis story, this "soul" is part landscape, part body, and part persona of man's "being" nature, as in "he breathed into him and he became a living *being.*"[28] This being nature dies when it gets separated from its living body, the breath of life. That's what our Bible tells happened in the beginning of our history, just at the very start of his — the man's — story, which is the "subject" matter of the Bible account. At our Bible's beginning, the "man" was dead, i.e., disconnected. He just

---

[27] *The American Heritage Dictionary of the English Language* (Noughton, Mifflin Company)
[28] "Soul" and "being" are of the same nature.

didn't know it. The beginning myths tell what happened to cause his death. And then another flood comes and erases that beginning[29] time. This is why the problem in our nature isn't understood today, according to the story. And it's true. This is why "faith" is essential. But, for faith to actually be a positive force in reforming one's life, it is important to know what this faith believes and if it's true. If it isn't true, all the faith in the world will do nothing at rectifying the causes behind our separation and suffering.

So the man is dead in the beginning. His behavior caused a great flood that took the breath away from all mankind. His "being" nature, call it soul, was lost and then forgotten. Being, what does that mean? (We see now why the English began talking about soul; because soul made sense or sort of sense.) The "dead" man was the problem God sat out to fix after he first broke him. God and his partner did the flood, right? Now the God in our Bible who was going to fix the lonely and confounded man was Yahweh, the spirit of God who first hovered over the waters in line two of the book of Genesis. So the fixer is the spirit of God. (This is why the apostle Paul liked the spirit so much! But did he like Yahweh of the Old Testament who seemed to be especially hard on anyone who had anything to do with governance or leadership or even the priesthood?)

It was "being" that was lost when our ancestors decided because of knowledge that their partner in life, the body, was "evil." That's like saying "My mother is the devil!" This caused a great shame across the whole species, and those early herds of humans were literally kicked out of nature. I mean, nature is foremost the body, when we take our seat in meditation, that breaths with us, right? I know, to a lot of people, this "body" thing is a hard idea. Call it soul then.

This shame, true to itself, is in denial of the pervasive anger and hard distrust that our minds have against all bodies, and most individuals

---

[29] The earlier generations, childhood and boyhood. But these two generations are the connection to our life's history. That's the tragedy of the disconnect; we lose our connection to life itself. This becomes the ground of all anxieties.

are the least and last to be aware of the divide that keeps our human being nature in the troughs of suffering and loss. Our souls won't go there, really, to the body, I mean; which kind of explains why the whole Middle Ages spent so much time imagining what it was going to be like when a body dies and the soul no longer can avoid paying back all the suffering it caused in its actual lifetime. But those efforts at imagining all come out of a corrupted language of distorted images that can't talk about what it feels like to be alive in a sensuous body. Everything covered by this imaginative disarray is "out there," either in the past or coming in the near future. The second coming will not be like that. The second coming is an opening onto the inside, where there are riches, a new heaven and earth.

We were speaking of the second coming, right? This will be the return of the son of man, the second generation in our being nature, rising out of the ashes of mankind. I should say "dust" since that's the word Genesis uses. To look for this second coming, let's turn to Joseph in his account with Pharaoh, i.e., the "lord of the house," and his troubles, i.e., bad dreams. This is a window into the second generation of Old Testament times. And it's ugly. Drought and famine had devastated the land. (It's always forgotten that before the flood, the land was burn to a crisp. The flood was to put out the fires mankind had started *everywhere*. You do understand an indoor landscape when it's written about, right?) Nobody was taking care in the raising of the children! That means the souls were drying up and dying, our being nature evaporating! The pharaoh's dreams were about what happens to boys and girls when the body takes over and leaves our being nature high and dry because all the body's energy is going into growing our physical nature into full potential and maturity, easy to lose contact with all the wealth and wisdom of childhood, which, from the story of the Garden of Eden, we know was rich in gold and other precious stones. I'm referring to the first land in the Garden of Eden. The famine happens inside boys and girls in that prepubescent time prior to adolescence (the second seven years of life) and especially when fathers are absent or unheard of to help their children transition into adulthood. Biblically speaking, fathers helping their sons is a myth. "In the beginning," there were no fathers, the flood having decimated mankind and "being" had become arrested in adolescence or earlier. Mankind was the penultimate generation; it wasn't the goal. And I don't know how much has changed in mankind's head space around the idea of supremacy over the "natural" world across a large portion of males today, but I suspect a lot, especially in the new young adult generations. Adolescent power and exploitation is totally seen as not sustainable in today's crowded world. Unfortunately for "our" problem, which is foremost a problem with spirit, the one thing nobody can do is "save" another's soul. It doesn't happen that way! The way it does happen is to make environments save enough so that individuals aren't constantly having to watch their back and are free enough to inquire as to what's happening in their own heads and hearts with the hope of improving life *there*.

Our Bible is really about reassurance (Can you believe it?) and where the well source of life resides. Speaking of which, there's another story about a man our Bible highly praises and who has been grossly misunderstood. His name is Abraham.

I assume the old days were horrible, the days prior to the Bible stories arising into awareness in the souls of those early fathers as to what was happening right before their eyes. In those early days, mankind must have preyed on their sons like male lions prey upon their cubs. Not that they care where the cubs came from or who fathered them, it's just the thing male lions do. What I'm assuming is that early human families weren't cohesive or the norm, and so this makes Abram the exception. Abraham was a shepherd and a nurturer. This was the difference and why he's in our DNA, in the beginning of our "being" nature at the beginning of this latest iteration in the lineage of *Being*.

We do remember that the man who was placed into that Garden of Eden had but one injunction pinned to his hairless chest, to cultivate and nurture his garden, which was also why he needed someone to help him because doing that alone was impossible. His nature (*our* nature) is a partnership like God and spirit are a partnership. Being is but a portion of what constitutes living. But a very important portion, being is the nature of "I am" and comes in different generations. The garden is the land of the four generations[30], the four evolutions of the soul (childhood, boyhood, adolescent, and fatherhood), and the garden was also the man's delight (Eden means delight). So his job would be his personal delight, if I use the meaning of the word Eden to stand in its place. When he was driven off that land, his care and delight were lost. His (our) delight was lost with our nature. From our Bible's perspective, making it to fatherhood, the fourth generation, was also the only activity that will ever have real meaning for him and his kin. This is where Abram succeeded. Our being nature was made to serve our partner nature, so a return to it guarantees delight.

The little that I know of as to what's going on today, in religious circles, as to what is being taught about scripture, is nothing of what I'm speaking about here. My experience in trying to discuss this with most all committed Christians, priests especially, is silence and sometimes a look of perplexity or irritation. It seems to remain unrecognized that our Bible is the sole problem keeping peoples from being reborn back into life. Human beings are far from stupid and blind, if truth be told. If they appear naive or ignorant, it is solely because those souls have been disenfranchised and manipulated by the powers that be, including the religious hierarchy. The tragedy is it's not hard to grow into a new life, with a new understanding, but the truths of our Bible have to be enlightened into pathways of personal practices. When that happens, the past traumas will heal.

Let us return to Abram and what he did with his son Isaac. Abram saved Isaac's life in more ways than not taking the life from his body. He saved him from guilt and shame. What had happened before this trip went down on the way to Mt. Moriah? Ishmael had been expelled from the Abram household. This was to protect Sarah's son Isaac. We know what happens when the child isn't protected from the elder sibling, like what happened to Abel. We also know what happens to the soul of the

---

[30] For another image of these four generations, see Revelation 4:7. Whether anyone looks or not, let me tell. There are four animals surrounding the child. The third animal had a *human face*, and the fourth was a *flying eagle*. The promise entailing a return to this nature, in the fourth generation, is freedom. Freedom means the end of suffering, the return to delight!

sibling that survives, like Cain, forever torment and suffering, to put it correctly, hell *on earth.* In this case, the guilty one is Isaac for having separated from his brother. He was the survivor. He should die for his sin because that is how he now feels without his brother. He feels dead.[31] His father took the blame away from him, thus saving his "being" life, temporarily until he could get a new partner, which will be the wife of his breathing flesh body. Wife, the original name before religion got involved, is the spokesperson for the living body.

When the man and woman were divided into individuals because of the knowledge of good and evil, the disease was picked up by the children. This division in the children was between the first-born, the natural heir of flesh and blood origin, and the second-born, the one who came to the knowledge of soul. One was strong and all body, like Adam, and the other was wise and full of thoughts, like Abel, the good shepherd. But with the coming of historical times, the two were no longer together. This is foretold in a line at the end of the flood account when Yahweh said, "Never again will I curse the earth because of man, because his heart contrives evil *from his infancy.*" The knowledge that flesh was evil had crept into the children. Their *own* body was their problem! This was termed "origin sin" by Augustine, the original sin of our thoughts, i.e., knowledge.

So after the angel stopped Abram from killing his son, he eyed a "ram" caught up in the bristles of its own truth. (Ram, in Egyptian iconology, was the personification of the highest striving of mankind.) It was the ram that Abraham put into the fire. His name, Ab-ram, means the "father" of the ram! This is why the New Testament makes so much of his name. He preceded the Christ by putting his own creation, the ram, into the fire and, thus, not just saving his son but also saving the whole of our being nature. And for this deed, he's given a new name, Ab—Ham. He becomes the father of the Ham lineage, which embodies

---

[31] In the Cain/Abel story, we have one who feels dead all the time and the other who hates his life so deeply that he wishes he were dead and all because they're not together. In the kingdom of being, there's nothing but ignoring that keeps the being world in disarray. As Buddhists rightly put it, the only problem with humans is ignorance.

the four generations of beings, after the garden. Only one name from the garden plot is carried into Ham's direct descendants, and that is Cush[32], but now a new light has been once more shone on our being nature. That light is Abraham. You see, long before the beginning, our being nature was shrouded in the dark. Even the first day of creation was half night, meaning that this new nature was making things even the eye could not discern. Ham means black, obscure, dark. Our being nature comes from the dark and lives on the inside, but it is the bright light of life itself. The hope in our Bible and for people everywhere is to bring this revelation into the light. The revelation of our Bible is that creation is all about "coming into being." It's not about babies!

See, the problem arises because our being nature develops over time and through different body configurations, like the first generation when we are babies, in small physical bodies. We're babies for a long time, and in all that time, our souls are being formed and informed and molded and bent into whatever our parents and the place we grow up in plant there through the child's experiences and how these factors force upon us those characteristics we needed to get along and survive and that we had basically nothing to do with, except ingest and become—the first generation! Then we became boys and girls growing up now in a larger environment and with more different parents because we are more different from when we were babies, and then the hormones come on, and everything gets crazy—the second generation!

The man in the Genesis account is a teenager, the third generation. The third generation is when the flood comes.[33] This is where the Bible begins, after the flood. This is where all the suffering starts and then grows. We still haven't fixed a thing. What we've been running on is a corrupted imagination and a need to escape, and that has created the whole world we live in today—the best of times and the worst of times!

So the second coming is the reawakening of the boy/girl generation into the physically mature bodies of the living adults of our worlds for the sole purpose of making "creation" good. But this awakening doesn't

---

[32] Havilah is there also, who is recounted to be the second born of Cush.

[33] "However, a flood was rising from the earth . . .," Genesis 2:6.

happen alone; who awakens in the adult is the long-awaited "father" who has lived his whole life in heaven, and this father, not unlike some of those big adults who might have loved us as we grew up, goes back into *my* second generation and rights all wrongs, heals all hurts, and restores all broken parts, like heaven now coming back down to earth and to the boy or girl we all know so well once we re-cut through all the smoke and trauma that surrounded us as we struggled at growing *up*. At least that's the promise in the name Jesus Christ.

When I look at the New Testament and all its accounts, I begin to wonder how much was even then understood and by whom and what percentage of the people.[34] Religion has always been weird and still is, but the hopes and the promises in our Bible are based on wholeness and integrity, even if a lot of the traditional practices are very dubious. From reading some of the scholarship around the proper names of our Bible, I've come to see the power invested in language when meaning is applied to the word. The man gave names to all the beings so God could see his thoughts! Take the name Jesus Christ. Christ is the Greek word for Messiah of the OT. Messiah remains the hope of religious peoples everywhere. Messiah means "the anointed one." Kings[35] were the anointed ones of Israel, but the anointing goes all the way back to Jacob running away from Esau who wanted to murder him. Jacob was the first dreamer! (Joseph later would totally "out-dream" his dad.) The stories are about the actual remaking of our being nature from scratch, so to speak. When the visiting spirit promised never to abandon him (from Jacob's ladder story) on his life journey until this spirit had brought him

---

[34] Thomas Merton wrote in a little book published posthumously entitled *Opening the Bible*, "No one knows what the Bible is actually about!" Merton was special in so far as he was not afraid to speak the truth about the confusion surrounding the Bible's meaning, and other events of his world.

[35] Kings were the promise of offspring to Sarai and Abram, Genesis 17:15. This was to ensure the promise of success in the garden: "Let them be masters!" of this new creation. Kings are those masters.

back to the Promised Land[36], Jacob anointed the rock which was his pillow during the night of his dreams. The second generation is like a dream state, through the eyes of unadulterated imagination, and is the first efforts at coming out into the living world. This is the time of fully activated imagination, a vivid adventure into life itself. And if you were lucky or fortunate, this awakening of imaginative experiencing was well established before language took over and blocked the clear lens of imagination, making seeing a part of the head instead of sense.[37]

The promise of the second coming is a return to our original mind of a newly embodied boy or girl. And of even more importance, this original mind is what made the world in the first place; everything that surrounds us was made by *it*. This is who the Christ in his Gospels personified, our mind's imaginative, creative faculties, of the second generation, a son of man. Our world is really the imagination's creation. So in the process of returning, the "world" can now be redone, made over again at my own beck and call, a new heaven and earth. What religious experts have failed to recognize is that the power behind the "seven days of creation" in the beginning is the active role imagination plays in all people's lives. This is also an affirmation within experience as stated within those same seven days of creation, that coming back to your body and to being will prove, once and for all, that life on this planet earth, all life, is good. This life is here now, made by God and his spirit, but we can't turn to this goodness without returning also to being aware of living inside *my* own breathing body.

The other half of the equation is Jesus!

Jesus is another Greek word, but its Hebrew equivalent is Joshua. Same name, Jesus = Joshua. (Did the apostle Paul know that?) The name Joshua, who lead the fleeing Hebrews out of the desert and into the Promised Land, means: "Yahweh saves!" Israel used it when blessing

---

[36] The Promised Land (Canaan) is the fourth generation (Ham's fourth son), the one after adolescence. This was what was missing "in the beginning"; in plain language, a mature human being! That's the promise.

[37] That's what losing your body means, losing the direct sense experience. Buddhists call this "beginners mind," before language. When we lose this immediacy of sense, how can a mind know what is true? The short answer, it can't.

Jacob's sons, between Dan and Gad. (Genesis 49:38) You could say that Israel shouted out, "Joshua!" It is the spirit who saves the son and restores him to the father[38] of our being nature. So literally, Jesus Christ means "Yahweh saves the anointed one," if you can take the scholars' word for it. The problem in accessing and implementing this process is the current disconnect between mind and body that feels to me like just about everybody's historical dilemma. I mean language itself takes us away, causes the divide. Everybody (supposedly, according to religious traditions) can't wait to die because they know they're going to some next new place because that's what tradition teaches, right? Even unholy people are respectful enough to speak of parents or uncles or aunts or grandmothers and grandfathers up there in heaven just wringing their hands and anxious for all those poor souls on earth to join up with them in heaven. Although in John's Revelation[39], he has it that everyone in heaven is actually anxious and distraught because they can't wait to get back to earth in the second coming, and what's taking so long? So it seems to make sense that the reconnection given in the gospels is exactly the right solution. Pick up your cross and follow after Jesus Christ because you're in Yahweh's hands, along with your living flesh body. You don't have to tell anybody what you're doing. Just pick up and join up. That means reconnecting with your living, breathing body and find out how it feels to once more come back to what's actually happening around you.

---

[38] Something else happens. Metaphorically, when a soul returns to its living body, it experiences the love and embrace of its very mother, the deepest connection to life itself. This is a bodily experience and the return to incarnation! Our being nature is made from the incorporation of experience. Mind and body are *not* two; they are part and parcel of each other.

[39] Revelation 6:10, 11.

ONE FINAL THOUGHT

What does "Yahweh" mean? I just went to the Internet and looked to see what was there, and it was way more than I wanted. It was also ambiguous. I'll take Yahweh at his word: "I am who I am." Not sure where that came from, Exodus? I also remember, "He is who he is." My question is this: If Yahweh saves the anointed one, what's that like when I turn into myself to find my "Promised Land"? Who is Yahweh in this instance besides being "my" spirit? How do I behold him? About his name above, we're talking pronouns, right? I am, He is. So when it comes to me, to my body, there's but one alternative missing. You are! Coming back to my body for me is coming back to "you are." And healing begins with you. That's *not* me. In the practice of mindfulness that I was introduced to five years ago, in practice, you begin foremost by accepting whatever is going on right now, in and with and around your body and your mind. That is where you begin. You always begin right now. That "right now" is my spirit: you are who you are. It is also the state that I'm in. *Right now* is always the state I'm in. And by definition, this is life. So coming back to being in my body is coming back to spirit and to imagination and to my whole life. In the New Testament, that is "being saved." All that I have to do is learn to pay attention, and in that activity, I will clean up my whole existence, morally, ethically, and physically.

Our being nature is as old as the hills, a well-deserved cliche. It goes all the way back through all the mammalian lineage. There's a lot of wisdom and goodness in everybody alive. And what's most keeping this from coming into our lives are our ideas and thoughts that have never been examined and questioned, handed down, so to speak, across the generations. And there's a good excuse for not looking; even the idea of reflecting can feel dangerous. A lot of our beliefs carry a truckload of ancient emotions, fear foremost, but also anger, resentment, and shame. Just thinking down those lines can cause your stomach to ache. That's because for a very long time we've been going through a dead phase in our being nature, and it's hard to know the truth about anything. This is nobody's fault, except maybe the author of that nature, which, in our Judeo-Christian heritage, is God and his spirit. The fault all goes to the maker of this nature, who would be the Christ of the New Testament. This was why the New Testament was so important. He admitted it! "It's not your fault!" The reasons why it happened the way it did are there in the New Testament also. The son always does what the father wants. This encapsulated the dynamics of the second generation, which is the father/son time, the time after the mother/child time. It's the father who supplies the ideas the son is to bring into existence. But until the New Testament, it wasn't recognized that our fathers were teenagers and didn't have a clue as to what they wanted. Teenagers have never been the real fathers.[40] Now's different; the father that men can become is in our being nature. The payment the Christ pointed to was also the promise of life and more of it for everybody alive.

Pick up and grow up, begin learning *to be*.

---

[40] From the biblical perspective, throughout historical times and before, our fathers were adolescents. This is not a criticism. We are highly brilliant creatures, but we're also crazy. That OT male spirit was *mad* with vengeance and couldn't do anything but *kill*. And it's true, but we forget inside and outside are not the same place whenever the living body is denied its feelings. In the whole world, the world of integrity and maturity, there is no longer division nor inside/outside. Anyway, that old world is no longer now. Here and now is not *that*.

www.ingramcontent.com/pod-product-compliance
Lightning Source LLC
Chambersburg PA
CBHW051420250726
48655CB00003B/1151